This Book Belongs To

The Story About Tigger

by Cameron Pendergraft

Illustrated by Jennifer Tipton Cappoen

Text copyright 2017 by Cameron Pendergraft. Illustrations copyright 2017 by Jennifer Tipton Cappoen. All rights reserved. No part of this book may be reproduced or transmitted in any form or by any means, electronic or mechanical, including photography, recording, or any information storage and retrieval system, without permission in writing from the publisher. The only exceptions are brief excerpts and reviews.

Author: Cameron Pendergraft
Cover Designer and Illustrator: Jennifer Tipton Cappoen
Editor: Lynn Bemer Coble

PCKids is an imprint of Paws and Claws Publishing, LLC.
1589 Skeet Club Road, Suite 102-175
High Point, NC 27265
www.PawsandClawsPublishing.com
info@pawsandclawspublishing.com

ISBN #978-1-946198-02-0
Printed in the United States

To my grandchildren.

Tigger is a five-year-old, mixed-breed female dog that lived in a no-kill animal shelter for seven months—from August through February—before our family adopted her.

Tigger's experiences inspired me to compose this story for my preschool-age grandchildren.

This is a story about a dog named Tigger. She was a funny-looking dog. She had short, sturdy legs and a long, chubby body. And she had a big head with soft, little ears. Tigger had kind-looking eyes that were the color of chocolate.

Tigger had a family of people that she loved. She liked to run outdoors and play with squeaky toys. She loved to sleep on the soft couch.

She was a happy dog because she had
a family of people that she loved.

One day, Tigger's family of people that she loved started packing all of their clothes into suitcases. They packed all of their dishes into boxes. Then they moved all of their furniture into a big yellow moving truck.

Tigger sat quietly. She watched as her favorite soft couch was placed into the big yellow truck.

The family that Tigger loved put Tigger into their car. They drove her to a big building.

Tigger saw a fence there. Inside the fence she saw a lot of other dogs barking and running around.

The family that Tigger loved took her out of their car. They took her into that building. They left her there with all of the other barking dogs.

This scared Tigger and made her very afraid.

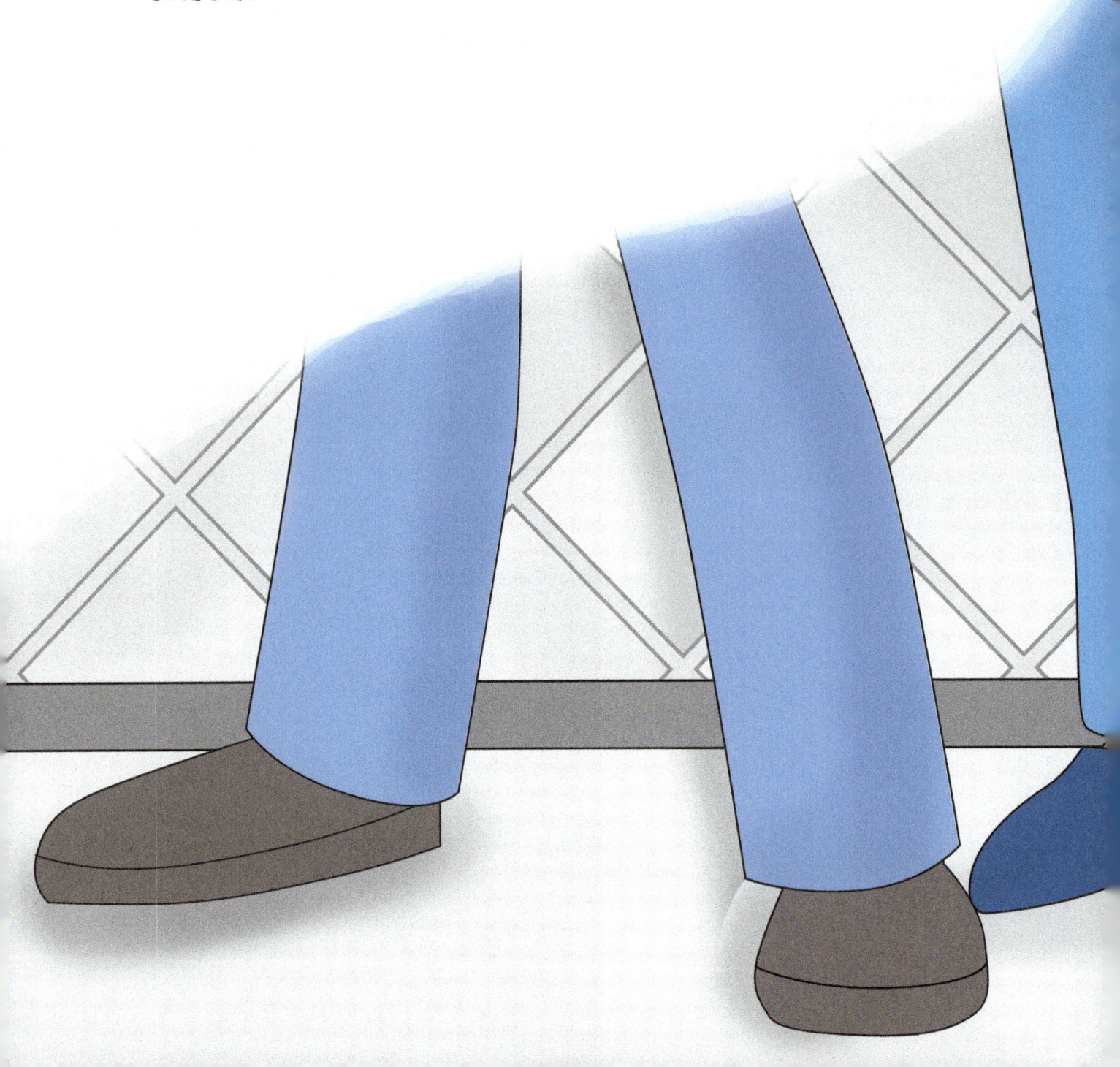

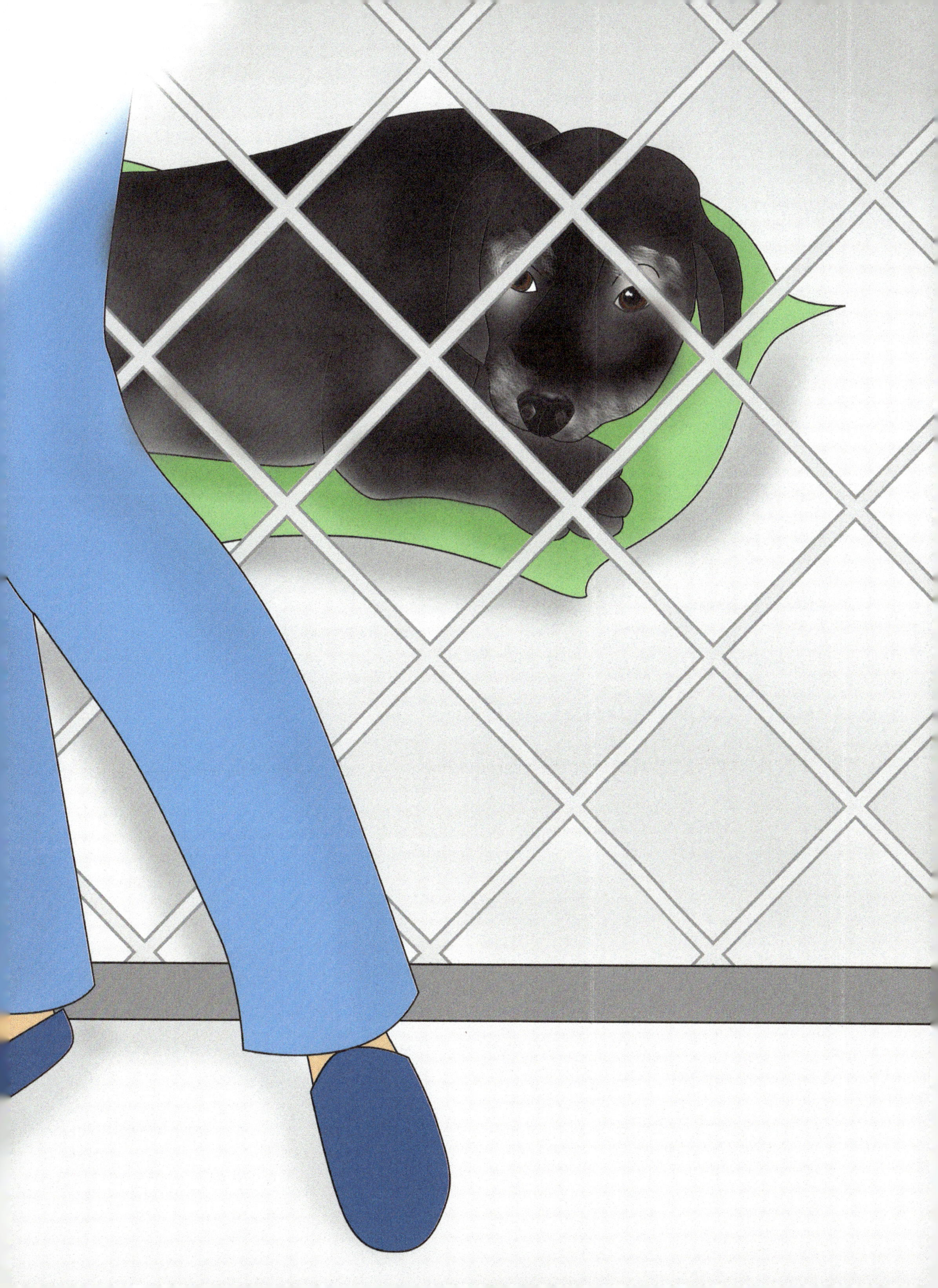

Tigger was put into a cage all alone. There was a bed. But there were no squeaky toys. There was a bowl of water, but no soft couch.

Where was her family of people that she loved? Why had they left her there with all of those barking dogs? Had she done something wrong? Tigger didn't understand.

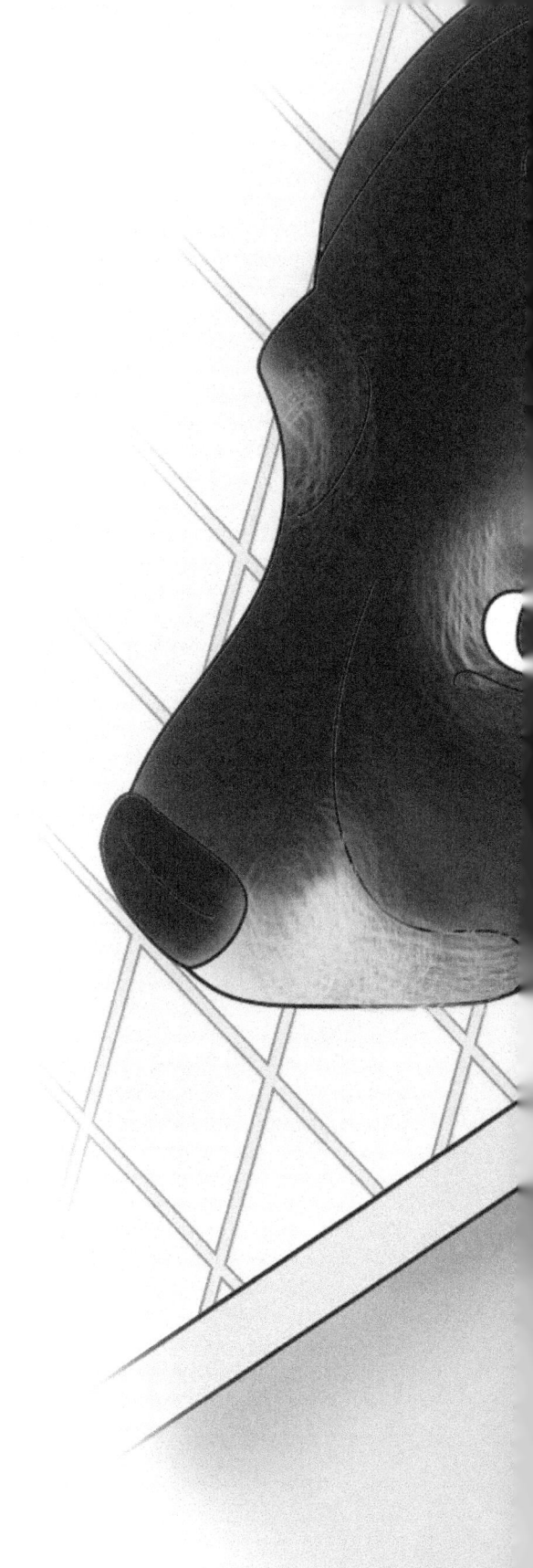

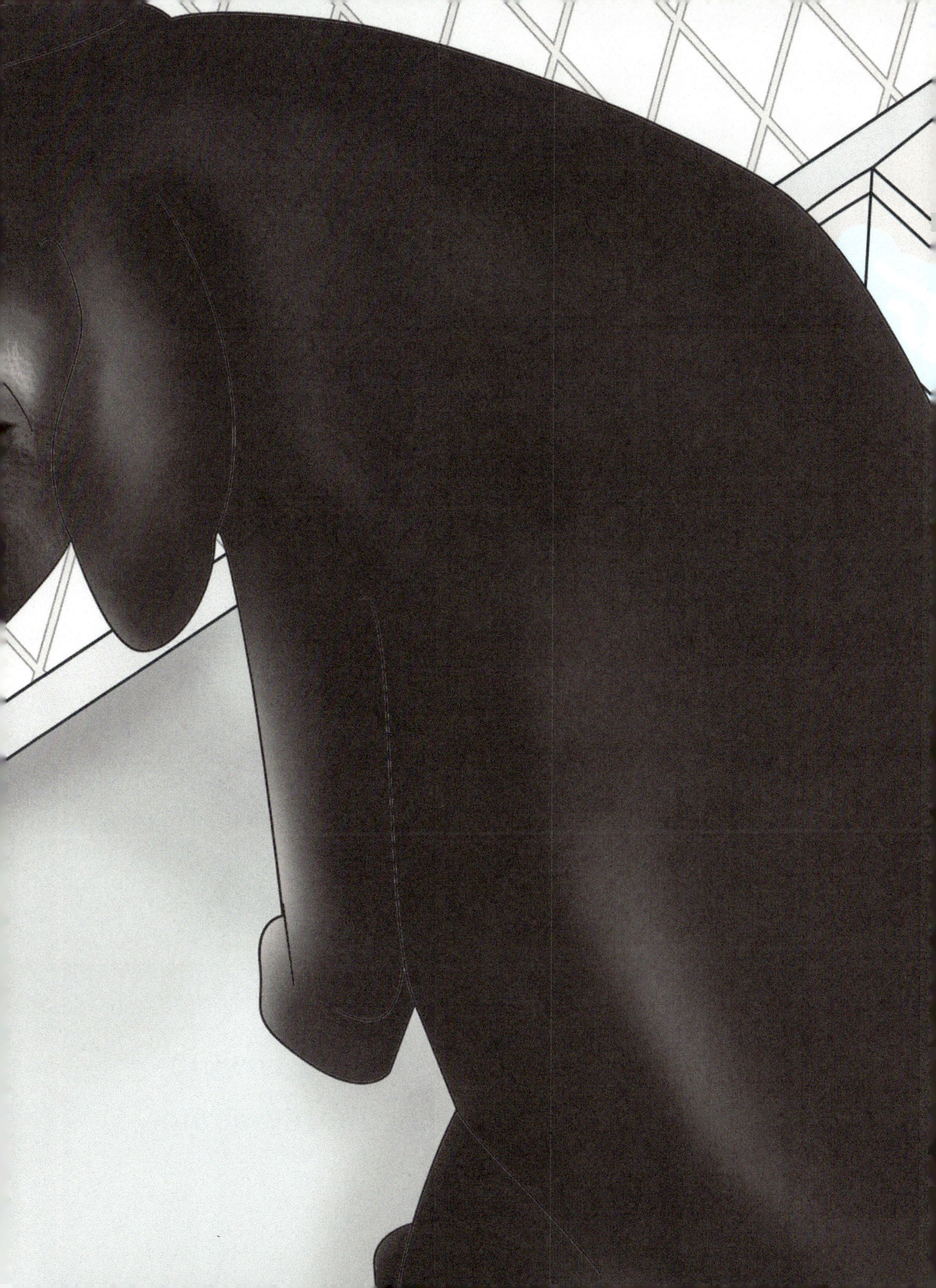

Sometimes there was a food bowl in that cage. And sometimes there was not.

There was nothing for Tigger to do in that cage. She sat still and listened to the other dogs barking.

For a very long time Tigger waited in the cage. She slept and she waited. She watched for someone to come and take her outdoors to go to the bathroom. Tigger would never make a mess where she slept.

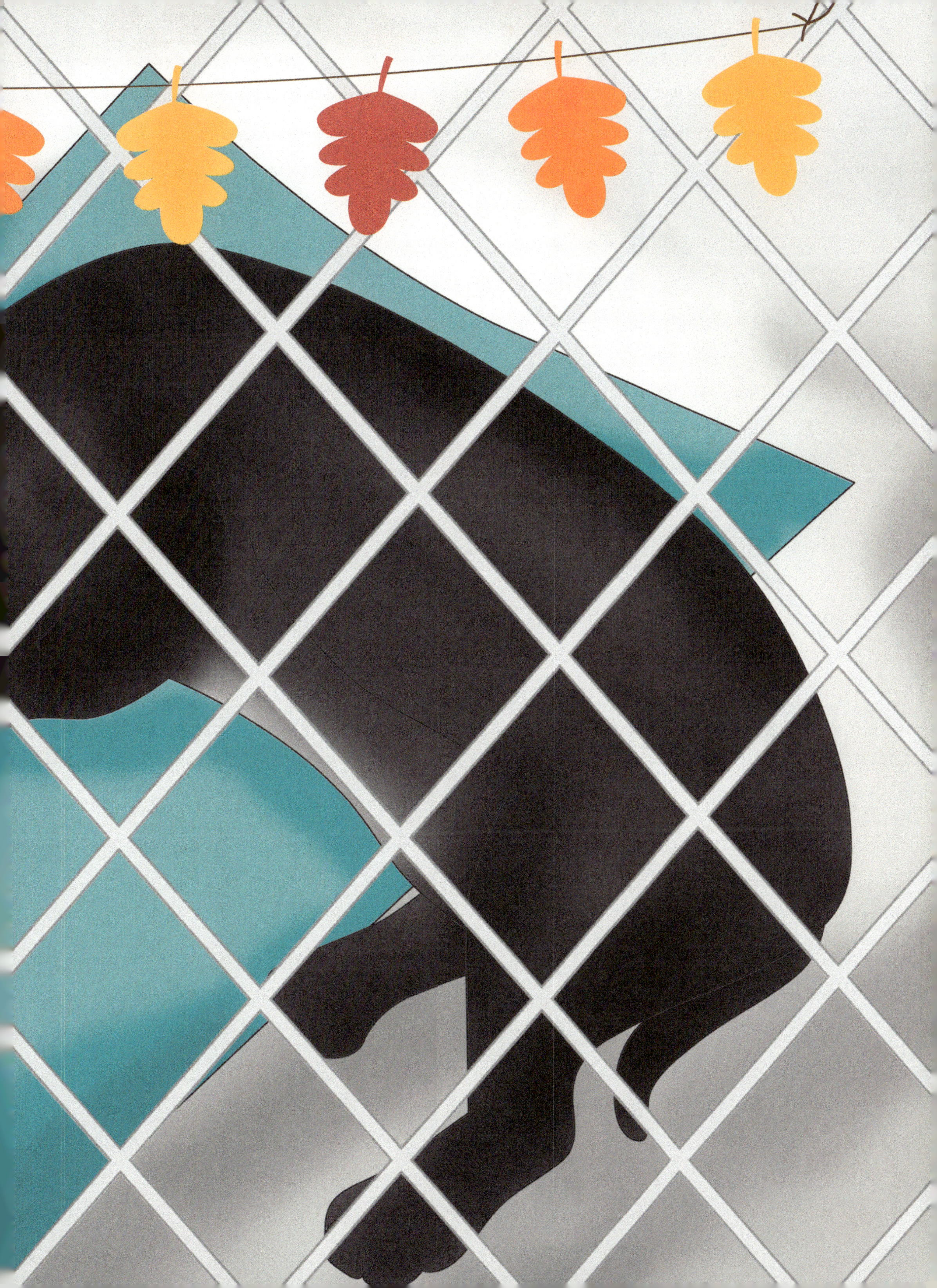

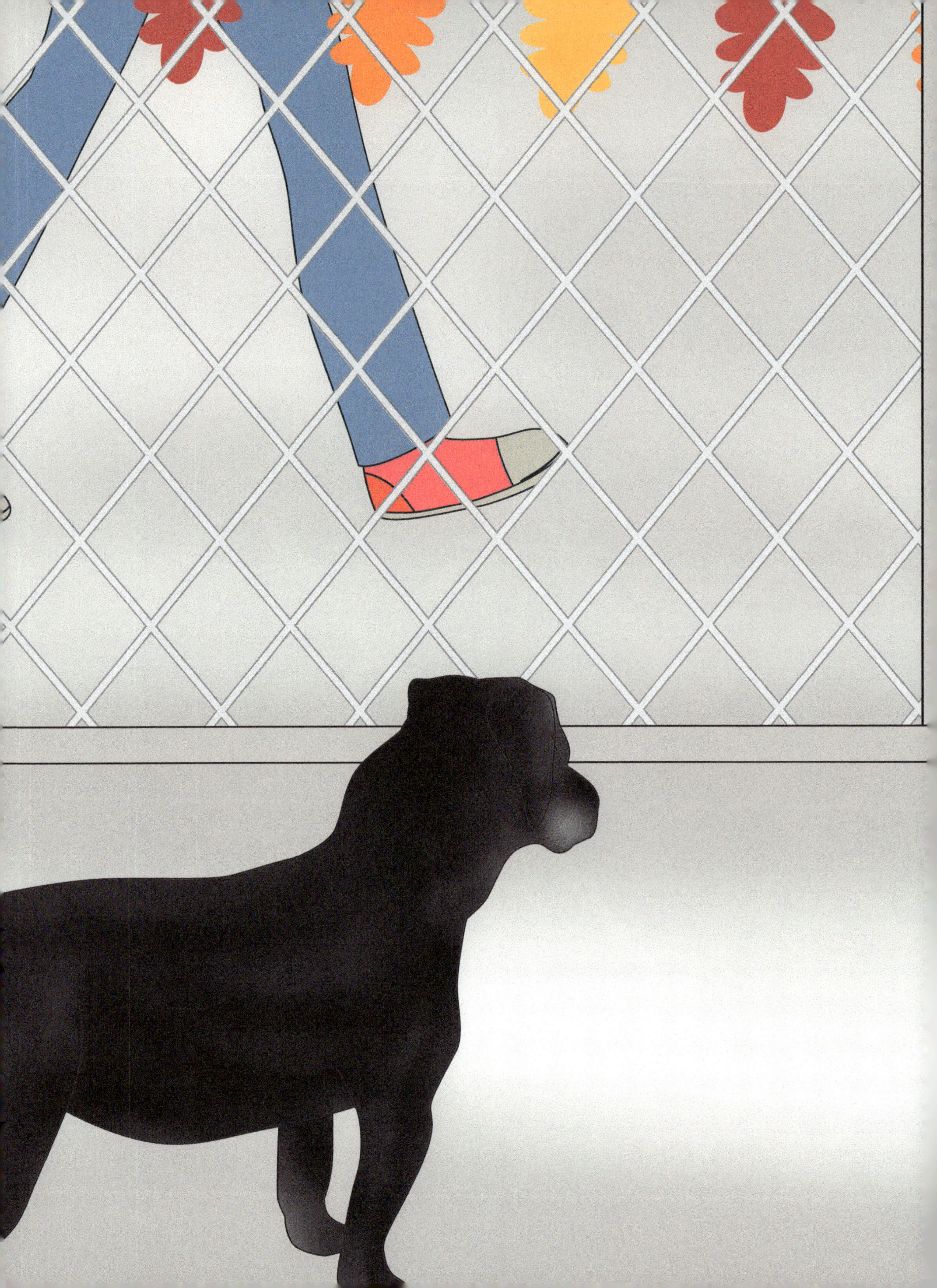

Sometimes people would walk by her cage, stop, and look. Some of them would speak to Tigger. But those people were not her family. Tigger waited for her family to come and get her.

Tigger was sad and lonely.

Tigger wanted to run outdoors. She wanted to play with squeaky toys. She wanted to sleep on a soft couch.

She just kept on waiting for the family that she loved to come back and get her.

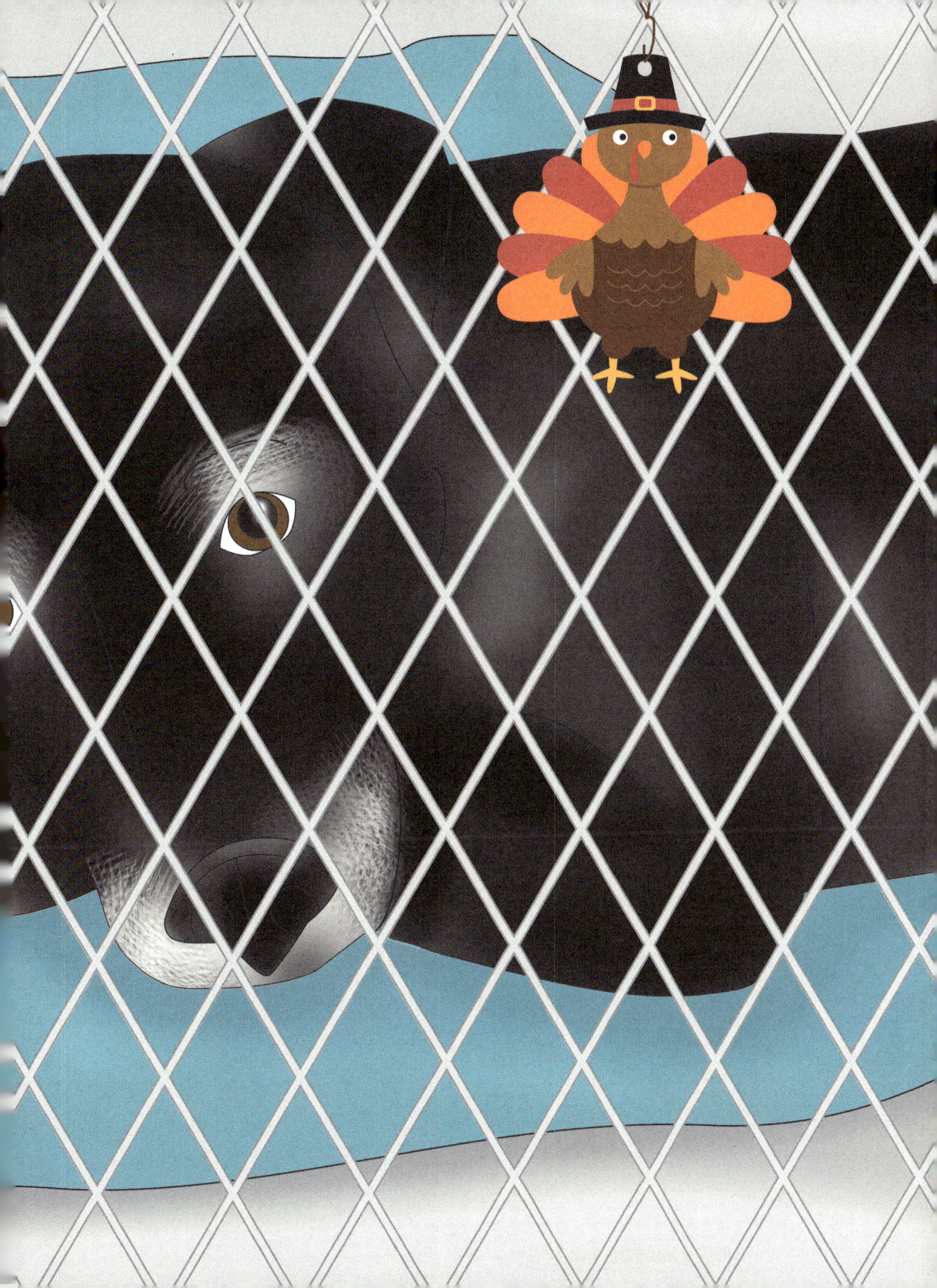

"She is housebroken?"

"She has such short legs."

There were people with many different faces who looked at Tigger in her cage. They watched her. Some of them smiled. Others looked sad. Sometimes they talked to her.

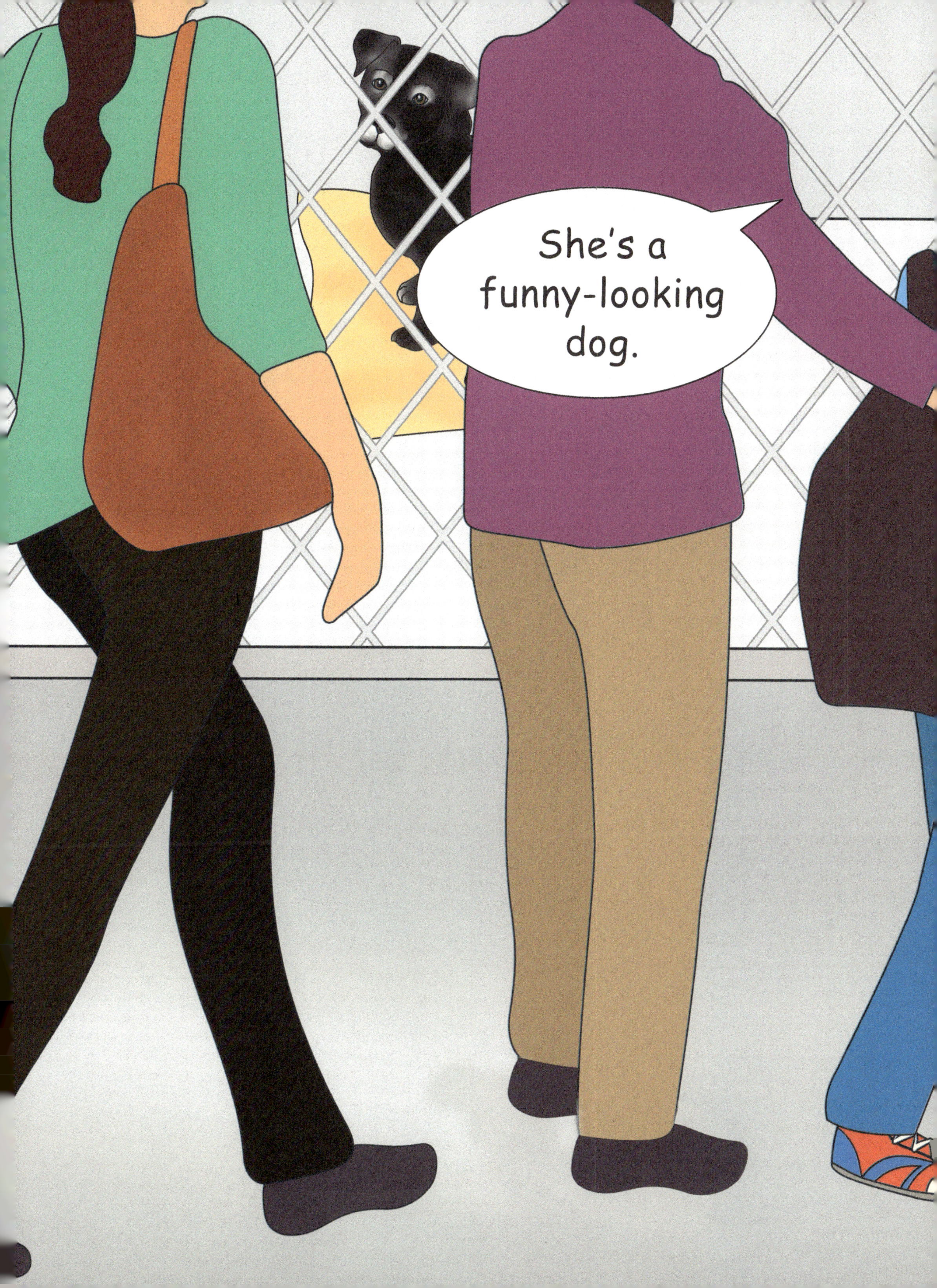
She's a funny-looking dog.

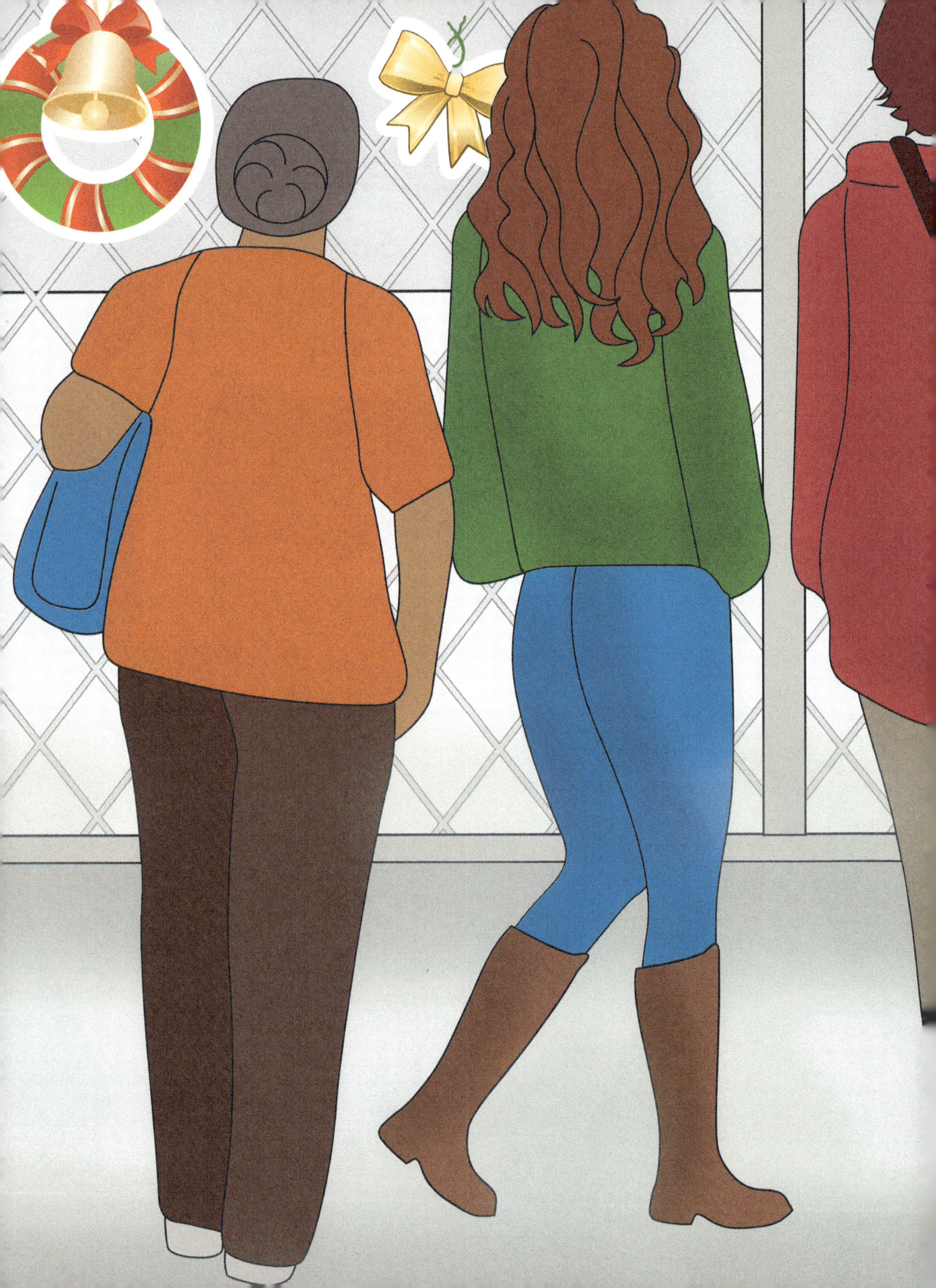

People stared at Tigger in her cage. But no one came over to rub her little soft ears.

No one told her she was a good girl.

Sometimes the other barking dogs left with people. The dogs that left didn't come back.

Tigger thought those dogs must have been very good dogs. Their families of people they loved had come back to get them.
Why didn't her family come back for her?

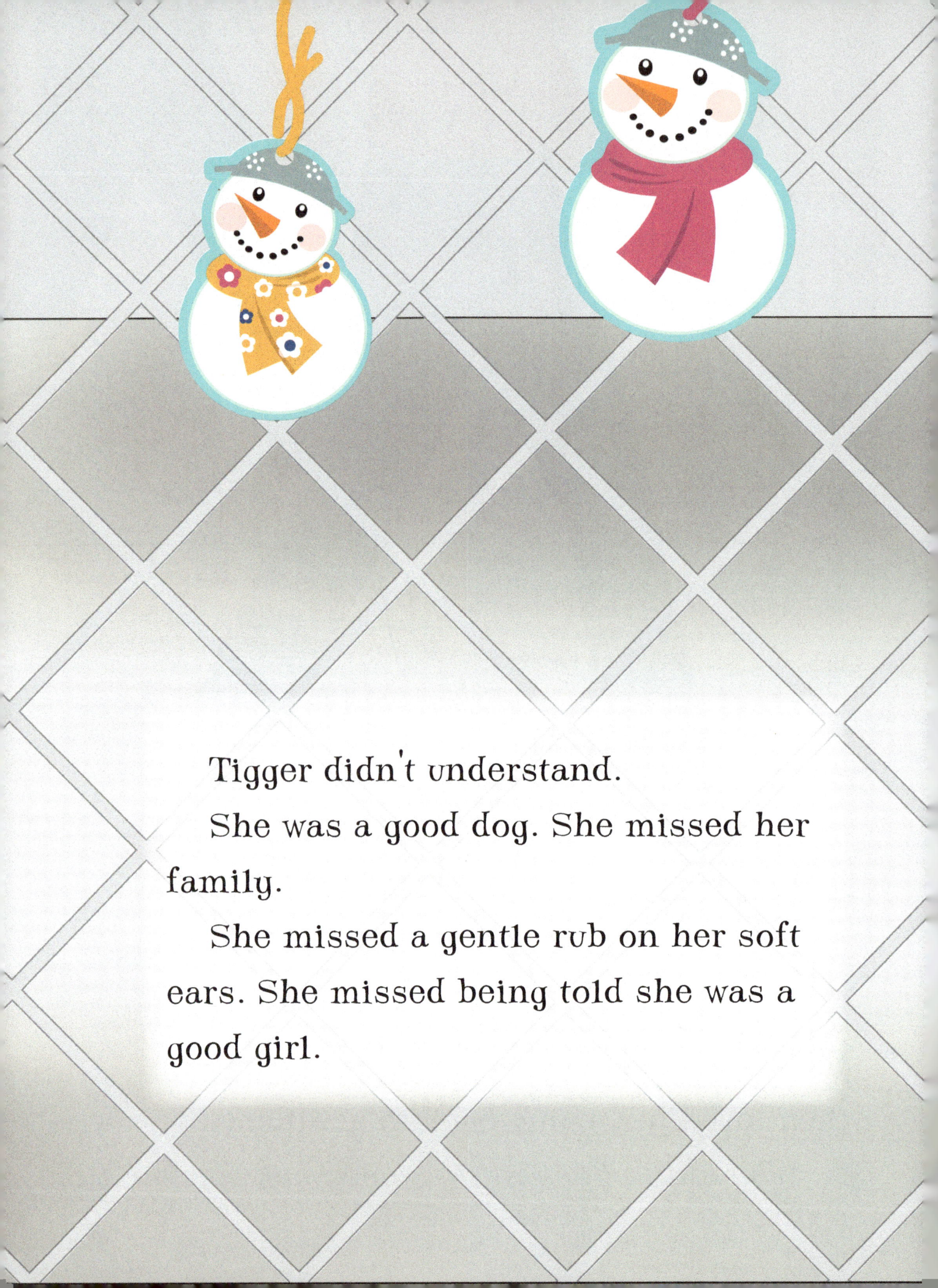

Tigger didn't understand.

She was a good dog. She missed her family.

She missed a gentle rub on her soft ears. She missed being told she was a good girl.

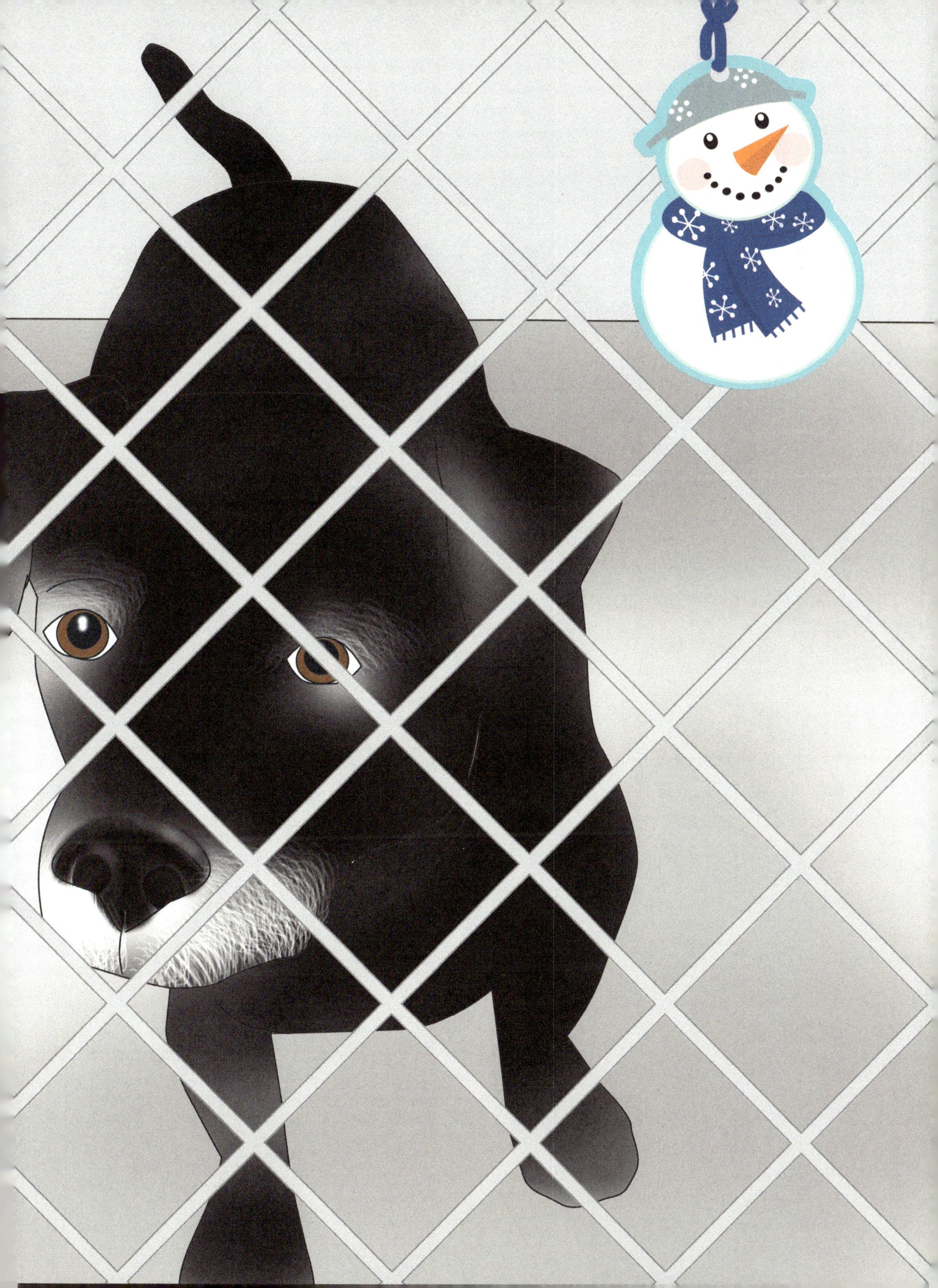

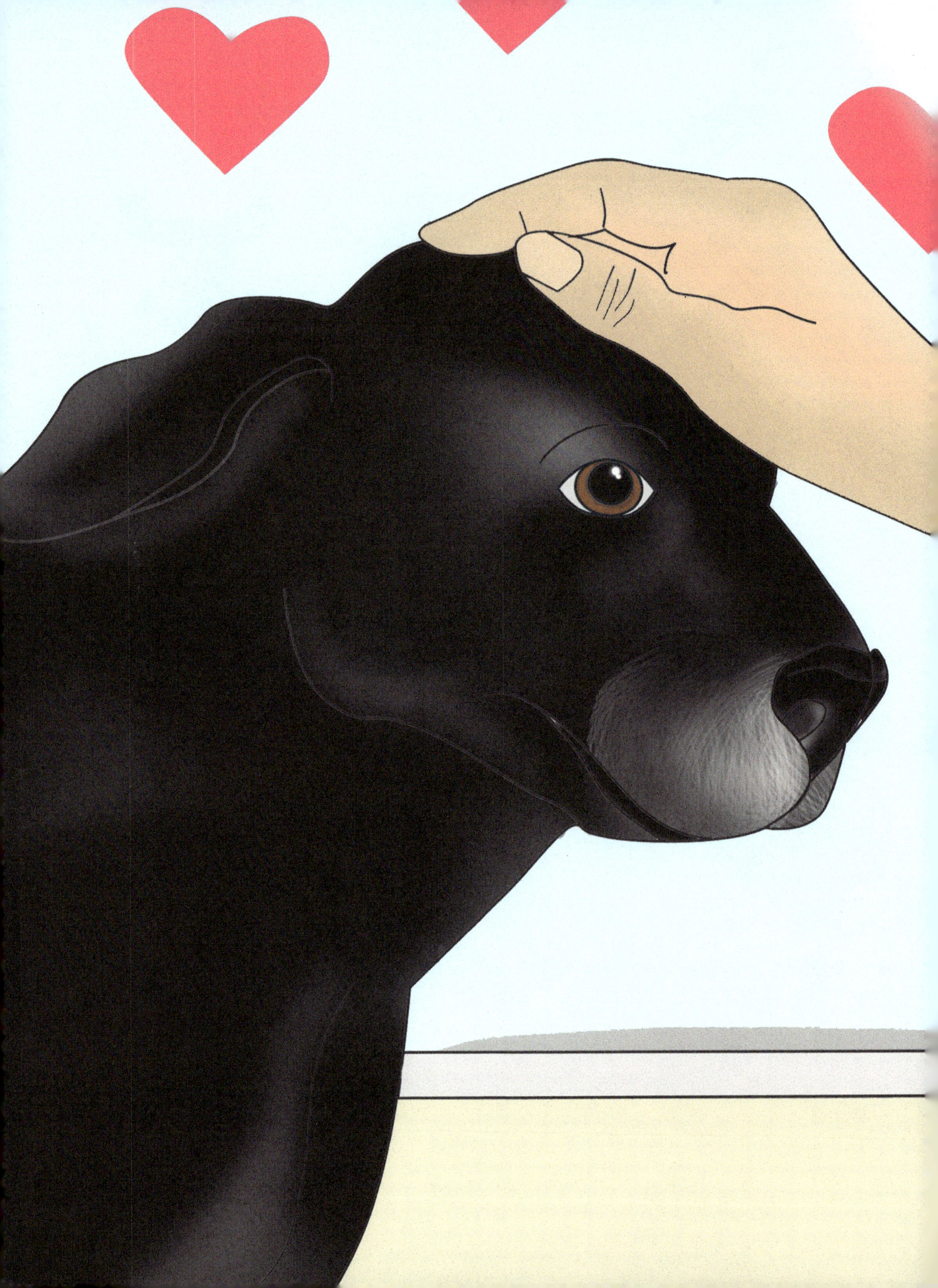

One day, a smiling lady opened the door to Tigger's cage. She looked at Tigger and said, "Hey, sweet girl." Tigger didn't look at the lady because she was not her family.

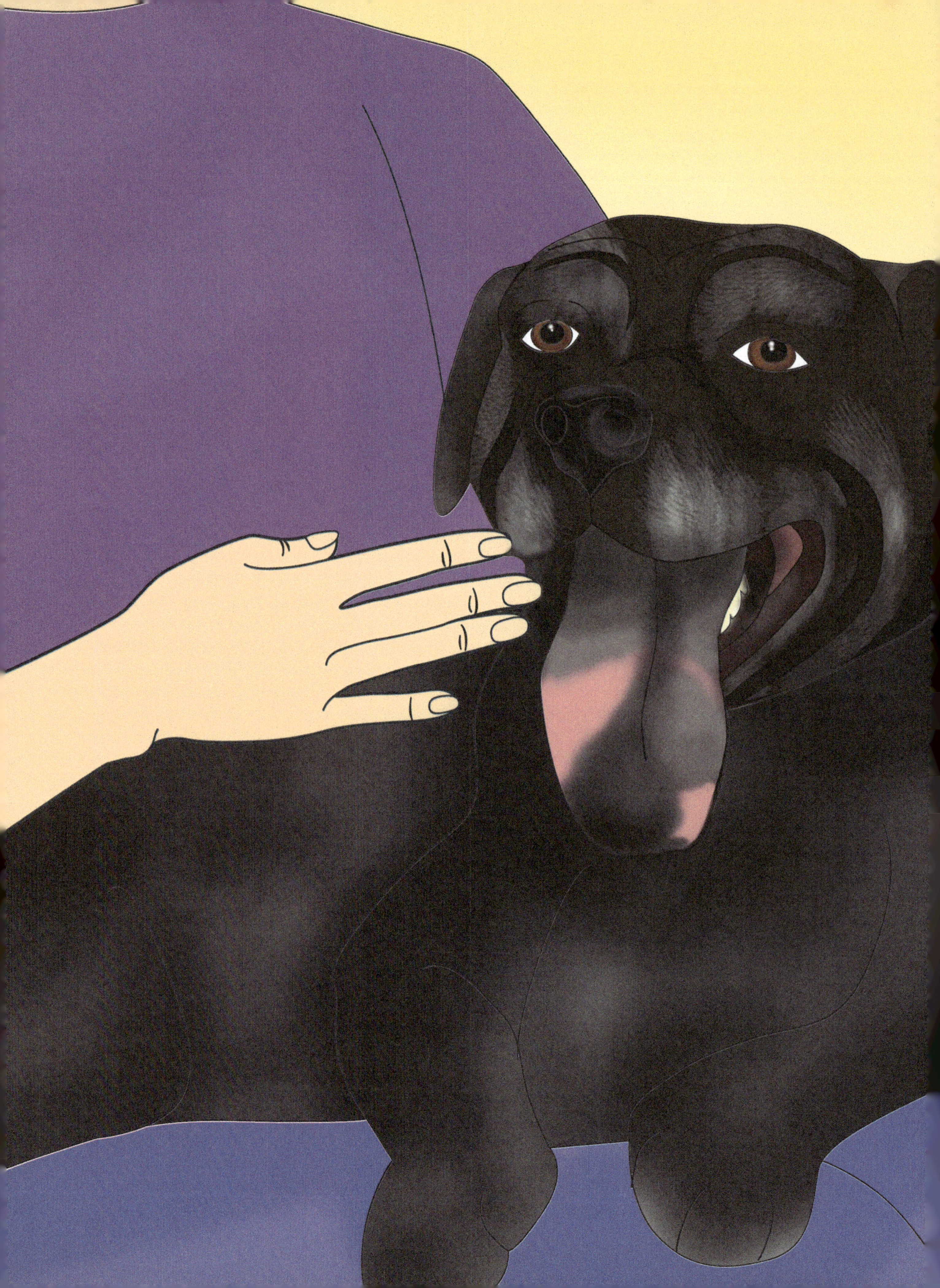

The smiling lady led Tigger into a big room. Tigger was alone with the lady. They were away from all of the barking dogs. And there was a squeaky toy!

Tigger got a gentle ear rub. Then she got another one. She found a soft lap to sit on.

Tigger was so excited because she felt happiness. She hadn't felt happy in a long, long time.

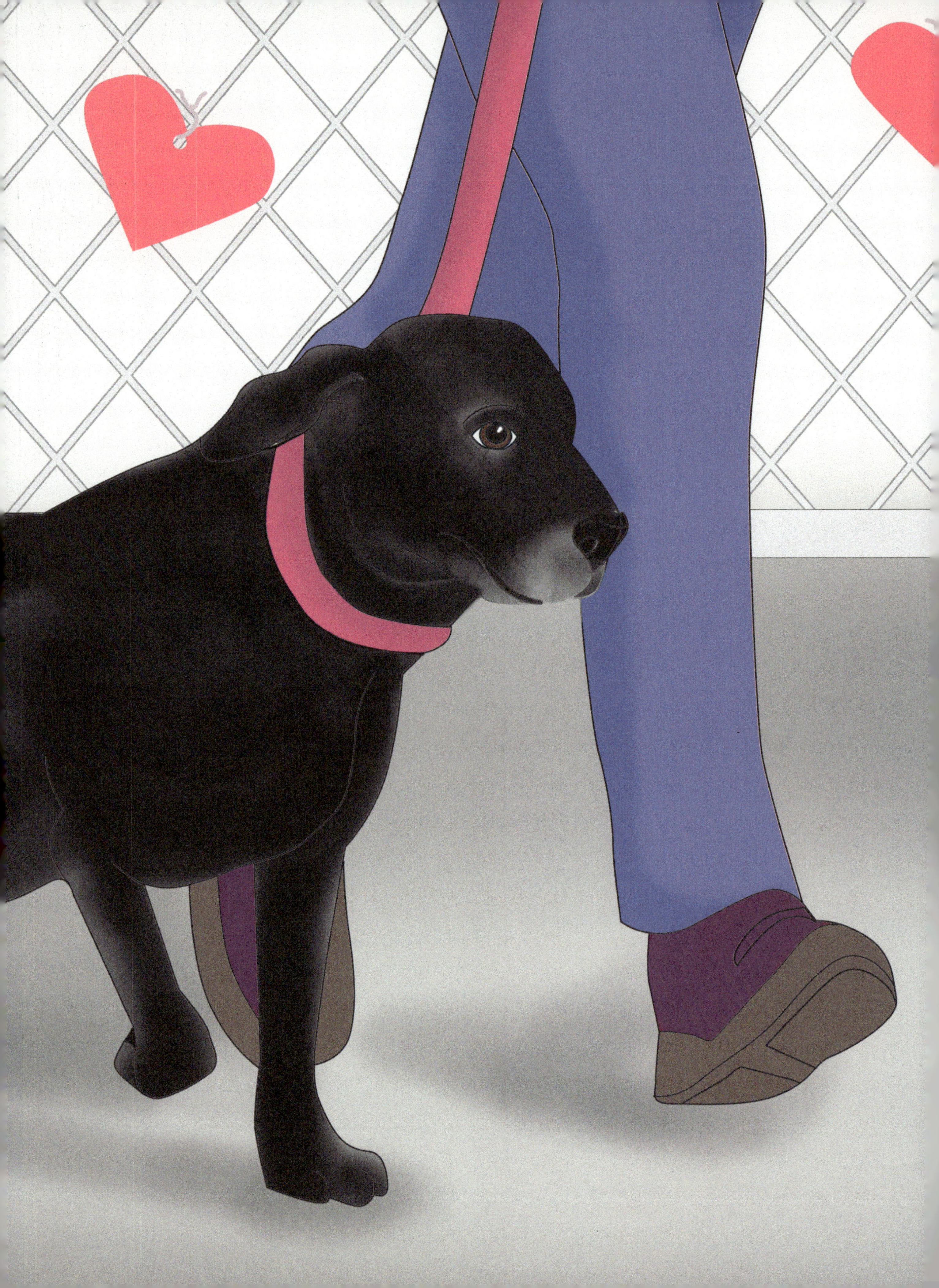

Happy Valentines!

The smiling lady buckled a bright pink collar around Tigger's neck. Then she hooked a leash onto the new collar. They walked out together.

The lady led Tigger outdoors to a big white truck. Tigger jumped into the backseat of the truck.

She stuck her nose out an opened window. Tigger hung out her tongue to feel the breeze.

She felt such pride and delight as the smiling lady drove her away from the building with the barking dogs.

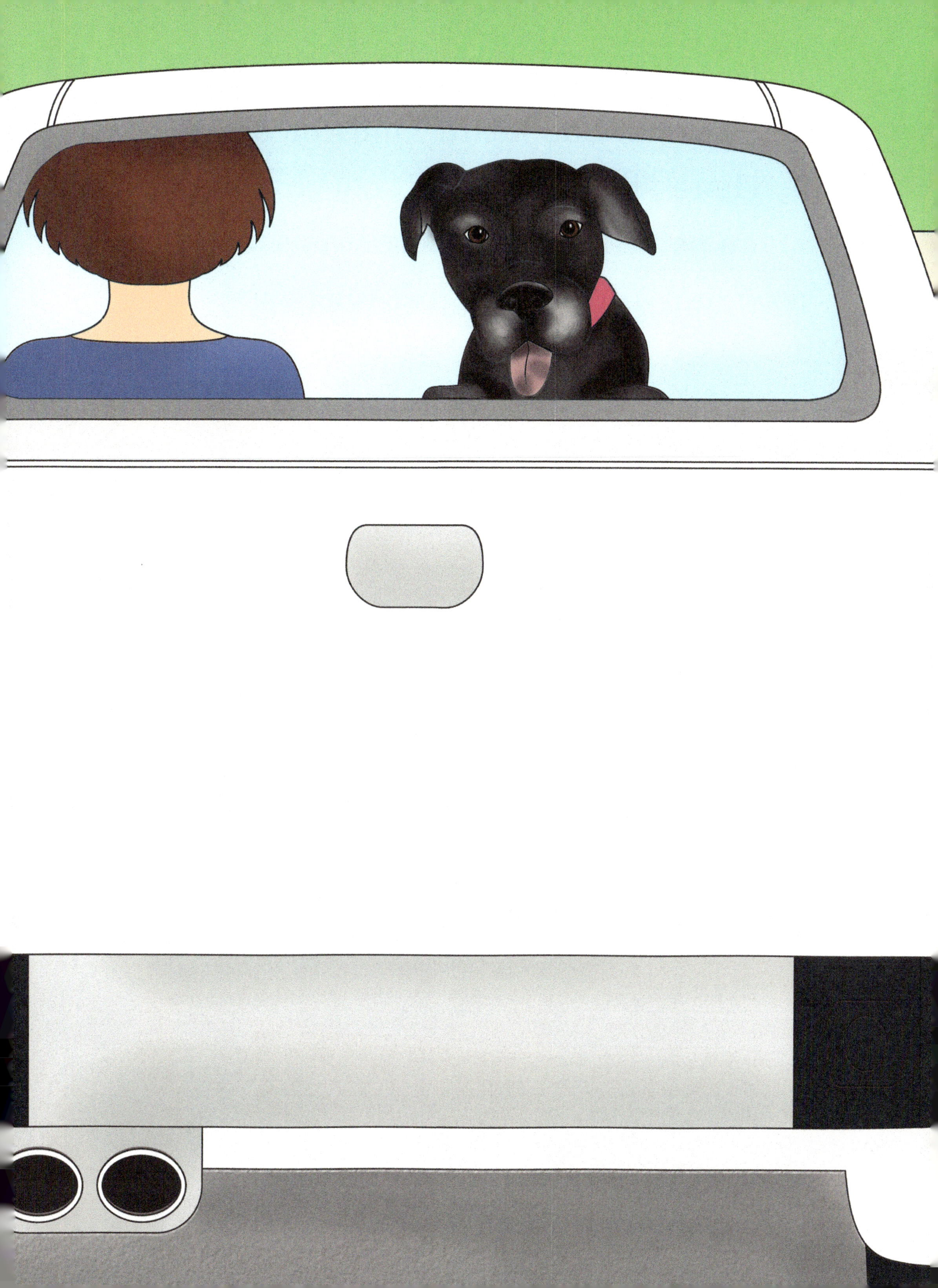

Tigger ran into the new house with new smells. She heard kind voices. There she found a soft couch and many squeaky toys. There was a water bowl and a food bowl just for her!

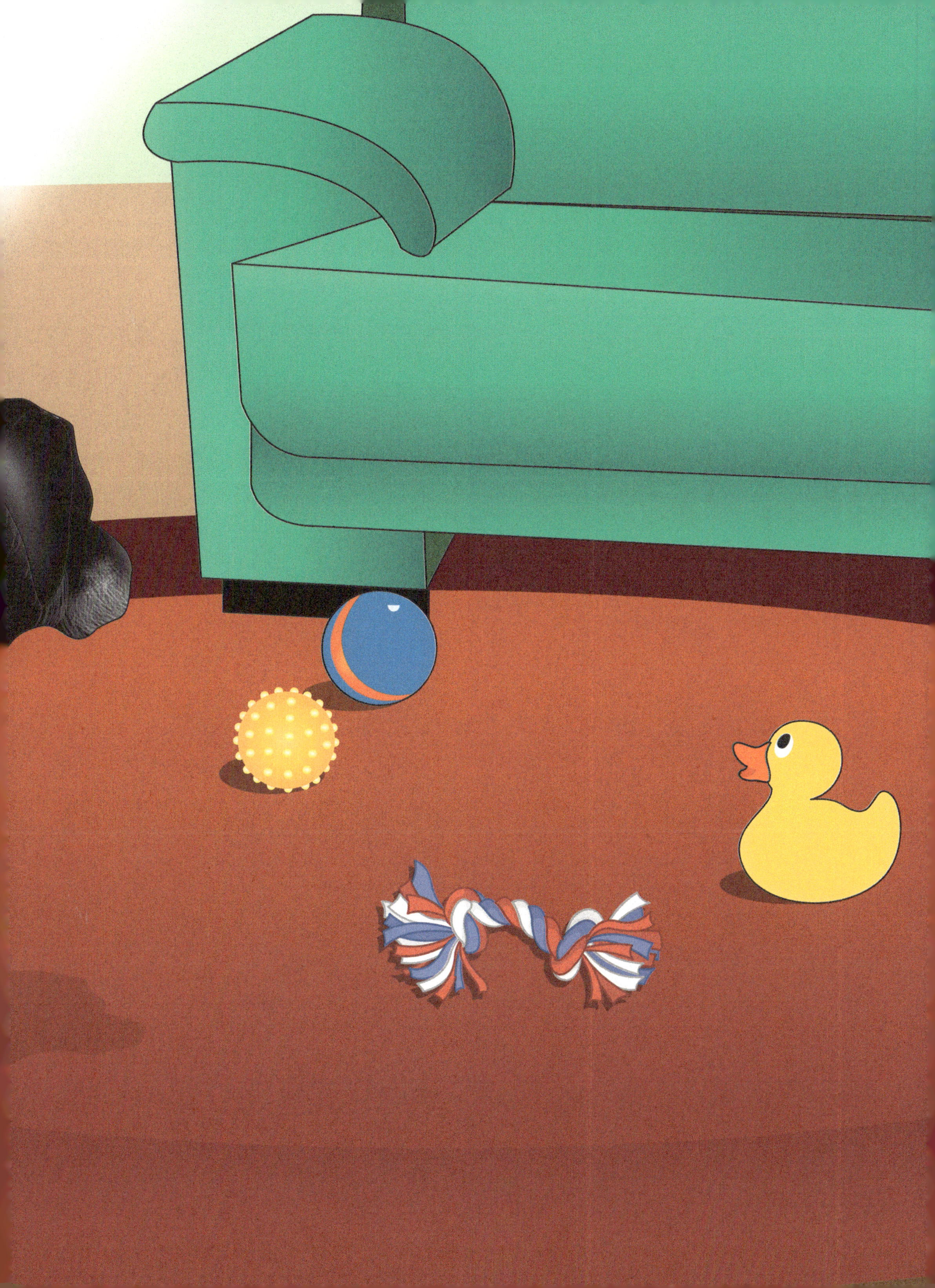

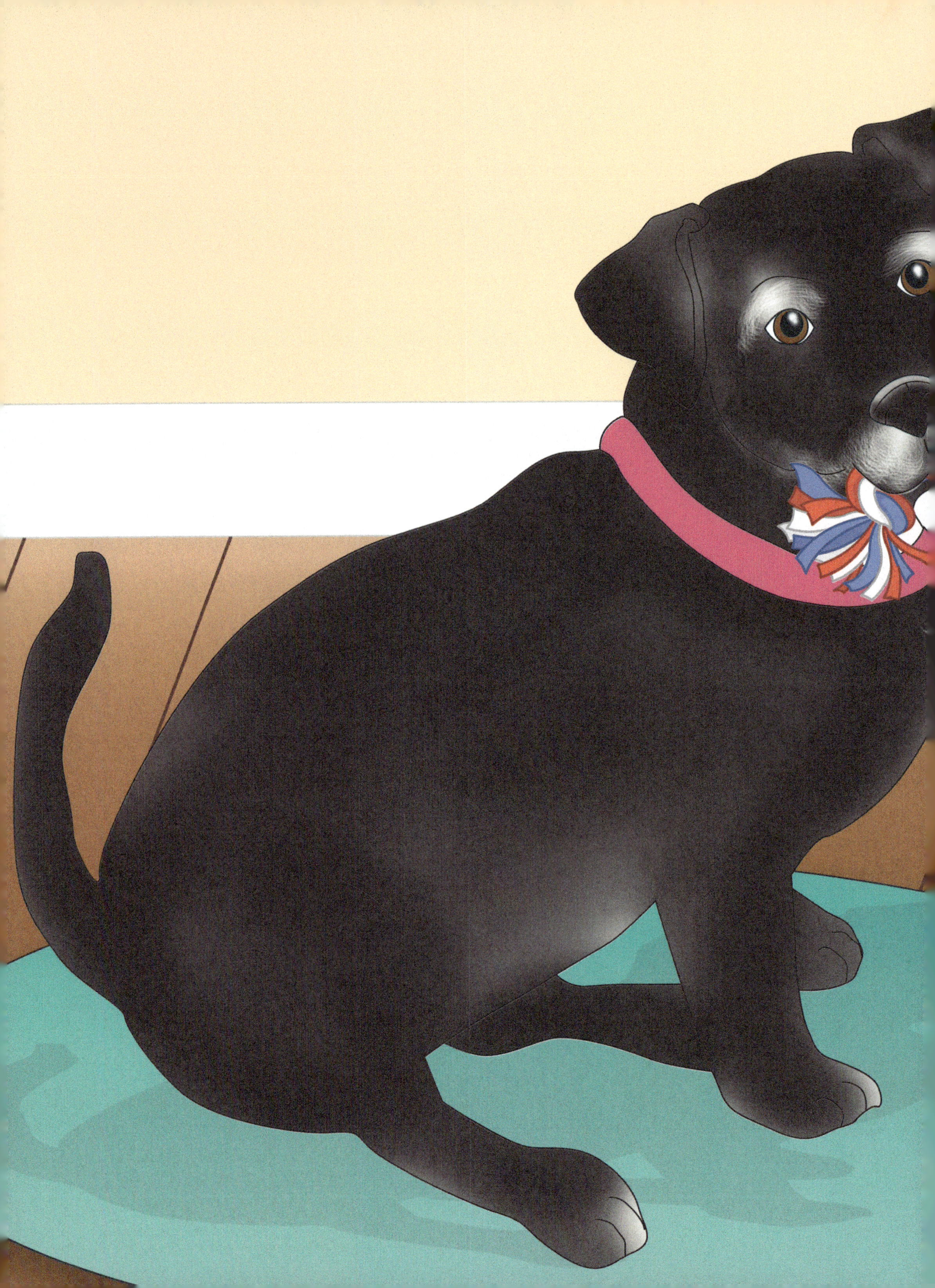

This new house was warm. These new people held Tigger and gently rubbed her little, soft ears.

They told her over and over that she was the prettiest dog they had ever seen. They loved her short, sturdy legs and her long, chubby body. And they loved her sweet-looking brown eyes the color of chocolate.

Tigger then understood that this family of people had chosen her! They seemed to care about her very much.

Tigger was once again a happy dog. She felt like she was truly loved.

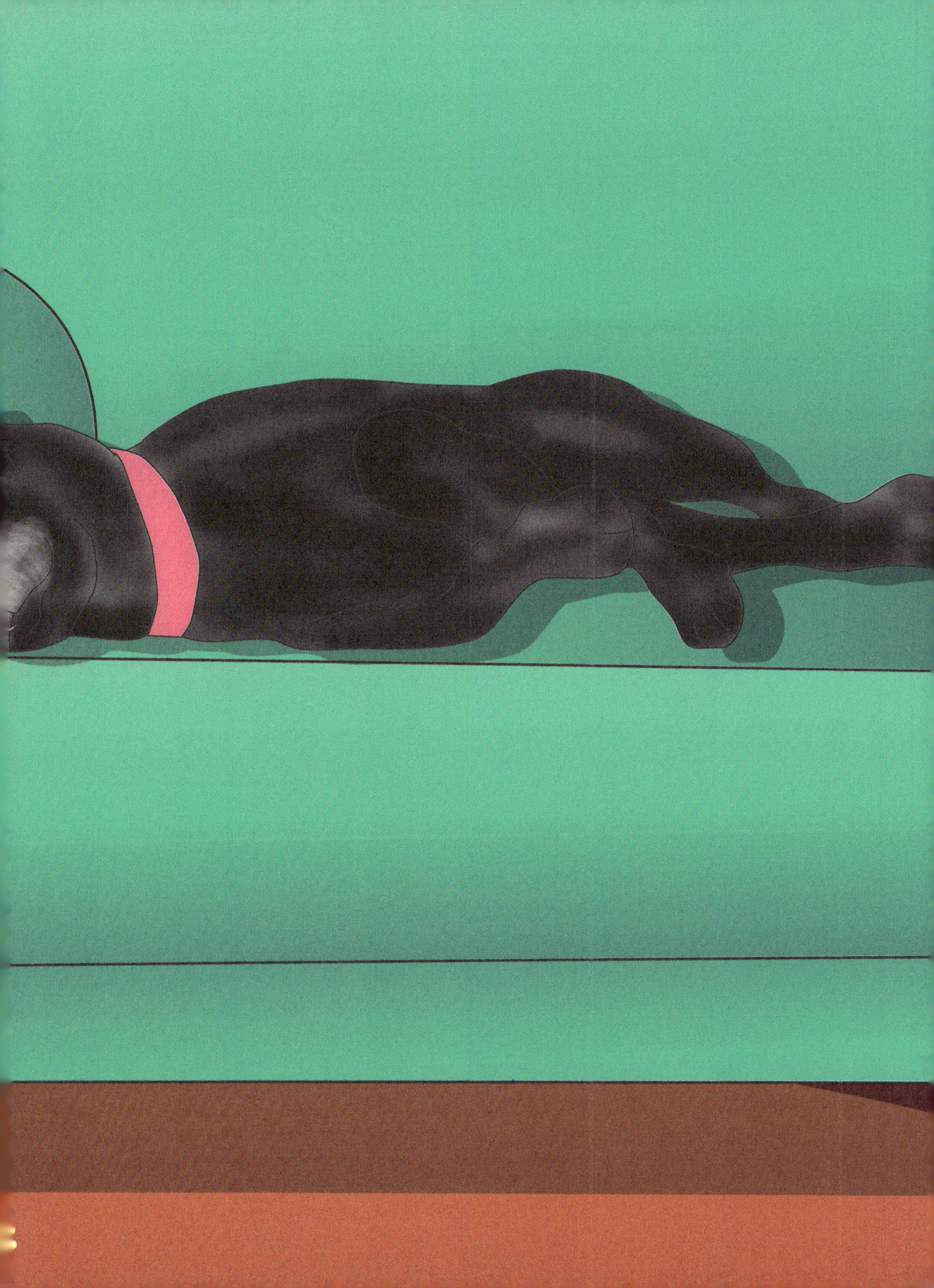

About the Author

Cameron lives in Oxford, North Carolina, with her husband Steve, their dog Tigger, and four cats.

The Story About Tigger is her first children's book.

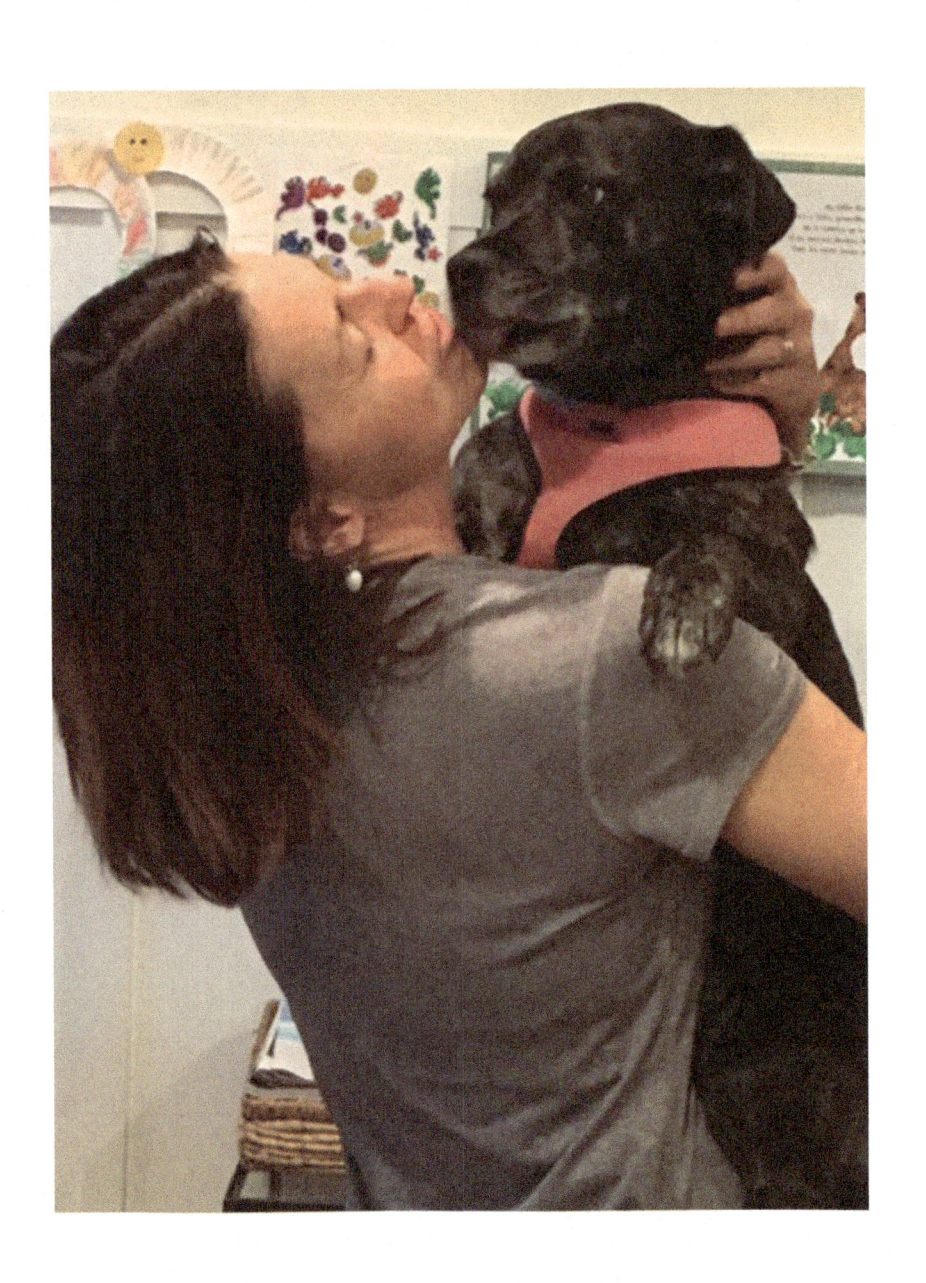

CPSIA information can be obtained
at www.ICGtesting.com
Printed in the USA
BVOW05s2121090317
478268BV00007B/9/P

9 781946 198020